This is a story about a little goat
who had no name.

One day the little goat skipped up the hill.
She sniffed the green grass
and she nibbled the green leaves.
But she felt sad.

On the way up the hill she met a man.
"Who are you?" asked the man.

"I'm a little goat,
and I'm all alone.
I wish I had
a name of my own."

"I'll give you a name," said the man.
"You can be Kitty."

"No thank you," said the little goat.
"That is the name for a cat.
Good-bye."

So the little goat
went on skipping up the hill.
She sniffed the green grass
and she nibbled the green leaves.
But still she felt sad.

Soon she met a woman.
"Who are you?" asked the woman.

"I'm a little goat,
and I'm all alone.
I wish I had
a name of my own."

"I'll give you a name," said the woman.
"You can be Blackie."

"No thank you," said the little goat.
"That is the name for a dog.
Good-bye."

So the little goat
went on skipping up the hill.
She sniffed the green grass
and she nibbled the green leaves.
But still she felt sad.

Soon she met a boy.
"Who are you?" asked the boy.

"I'm a little goat,
and I'm all alone.
I wish I had
a name of my own."

"I'll give you a name," said the boy. "You can be Mollie."

"No thank you," said the little goat. "That is the name for a cow. Good-bye."

So the little goat
went on skipping up the hill.
She sniffed the green grass
and she nibbled the green leaves.
But still she felt sad.

Soon she met a girl.
"Who are you?" asked the girl.
"I'm a little goat,
and I'm all alone.
I wish I had
a name of my own."

"I'll give you a name," said the girl. "You can be Curly."

"No thank you," said the little goat. "That is the name for a pig. Good-bye."

So the little goat
went on skipping up the hill.
She sniffed the green grass
and she nibbled the green leaves.
But still she felt sad.

Soon she met a sheep-dog.
"Who are you?" asked the sheep-dog.
"I'm a little goat,
and I'm all alone.
I wish I had
a name of my own."

"I'll give you a name," said the sheep-dog. "You can be Woolly."

"No thank you," said the little goat. "That is the name for a sheep. Good-bye."

So the little goat
went on skipping up the hill.
She sniffed the green grass
and she nibbled the green leaves.
But still she felt sad.

Soon she met a big goat.
"Who are you?" asked the big goat.

"I'm a little goat,
and I'm all alone.
I wish I had
a name of my own."

"I'll give you a name," said the big goat.
"You can be Skipper."

"Thank you! Thank you!" said the little goat.
"That is just right.
It is a very good name for a little goat."

Then the big goat and the little goat
went on skipping up the hill together.
They sniffed the green grass
and they nibbled the green leaves.
The big goat skipped with big skips
and the little goat skipped with little skips.
They were both very happy.